Wherever Home Begins

A RICHARD JACKSON BOOK

Also by Paul B. Janeczko

POETRY COLLECTIONS

Strings: *A Gathering of Family Poems*
Pocket Poems
Poetspeak: *In Their Work, About Their Work*
Dont Forget to Fly
Postcard Poems
Going Over to Your Place: *Poems for Each Other*
This Delicious Day: *65 Poems*
The Music of What Happens: *Poems That Tell Stories*
The Place My Words Are Looking For
Preposterous: *Poems of Youth*
Looking for Your Name: *A Collection of Contemporary Poems*

ORIGINAL POETRY

Brickyard Summer
Stardust   otel

FICTION

Bridges to Cross

NONFICTION

Loads of Codes and Secret Ciphers

Wherever Home Begins

100 CONTEMPORARY POEMS

selected by Paul B. Janeczko

ORCHARD BOOKS   NEW YORK

Orchard Books
95 Madison Avenue
New York, NY 10016

Manufactured in the United States of America
Book design by Jean Krulis
The text of this book is set in 10 point Meridien.
10 9 8 7 6 5 4 3 2 1

Library of Congress Cataloging-in-Publication Data
Wherever home begins : 100 contemporary
poems / selected by Paul B. Janeczko.
p. cm.
"A Richard Jackson book."
Includes index.
ISBN 0-531-09481-2. — ISBN 0-531-08781-6 (lib. bdg.)
1. Home—Juvenile poetry. 2. Children's
poetry, American.
[1. Home—Poetry. 2. American poetry—
Collections.] I. Janeczko, Paul B.
PS595.H645W48 1995   811'.54080355—
dc20   94-48740

for Jay
big brother
former hot rodder
who introduced me to the world of Acme
and took me to the Rainbow's End

Contents

Where I Live

WESLEY MCNAIR

You will come into an antique town
whose houses move apart
as if you'd interrupted
a private discussion. This is the place
you must pass through to get there.
Imagining lives tucked in
like china plates, continue driving.
Beyond the landscaped streets,
beyond the last colonial gas station
and unsolved by zoning,
is a road. It will take you
to old farmhouses and trees
with car-tire swings.
Signs will announce hairdressing
and night crawlers.
The timothy grass will run beside you
all the way to where I live.

Small Town at Dusk

JO MCDOUGALL

Cars on the bypass
move between places with restaurants
we have forgotten the names of.
Fireflies appear and disappear.
Night takes the sidewalks first
and then the marigolds and the sprinklers,
the children's skates.
Nothing argues with the ambling dogs
except the tree frogs and the occasional slamming
of a screen door.

The School

DAVID HUDDLE

On one side the high school, on the other
grades one through seven, the purple-curtained
auditorium shrank and grew shabbier
each August we came back. Mr. Whitt one year
decided Charles Tomlinson, Slick King, Dwayne
Burchett, Bobby Peaks, and Big Face Cather
could be a basketball team. They practiced
on a rocky, red-dirt court with a basket
and some boards on a post. They drove to games
—always at the other school—in Slick's Ford.
Uniforms were jeans and T-shirts. Big Face
and Bobby played barefoot. They lost by scores
like ten to ninety-three, unaccustomed to such space,
wooden floors, lights, adults calling them names.

Dragging Broadway

MARK VINZ

Weekends they line up for the parade,
in from every town for miles—
six blocks up and six blocks back,
while the city debates what to do about it.
The noise, the traffic, the threat of beer
and worse, much worse, they say.
You know kids, that trick of being seen
and heard.
          The tired cop keeps watching
from his motorbike—in every passing window
another face he knows. What's there to do,
anyway? Every week the circle dance grows
longer, each car braying different songs.
The words keep changing, too, the words
keep moving like a pulse, but every
now and then an old familiar tune—
until there's nothing left again but
empty streets and small lights burning
in the safe and songless dark.

Sunday Night in Santa Rosa

DANA GIOIA

The carnival is over. The high tents,
the palaces of light, are folded flat
and trucked away. A three-time loser yanks
the Wheel of Fortune off the wall. Mice
pick through the garbage by the popcorn stand.
A drunken giant falls asleep beside
the juggler, and the Dog-Faced Boy sneaks off
to join the Serpent Lady for the night.
Wind sweeps ticket stubs along the walk.
The Dead Man loads his coffin on a truck.

Off in a trailer by the parking lot
the radio predicts tomorrow's weather
while a clown stares in a dressing mirror,
takes out a box, and peels away his face.

Mississinewa County Road

JARED CARTER

When you drive at dusk, alone,
After the corn is harvested, the wind
Scatters bits of dry husk along the road.
A farmer has draped a groundhog's carcass
Across the corner of a wire fence
And the crows have pecked out its eyes.
Your headlights show these things
To a part of your mind that cannot hurry,
That has never learned to decide.
While the car goes on, you get out
And stand with the chaff blowing
And crickets in the grass at the road's edge.
In the distance there is a dog barking
And somewhere a windmill turning in the wind.

Mount Mitchell in North Carolina
at Dusk in October

THOMAS HEFFERNAN

Far ahead, the road curves through the blue trees
like the silver trail a boat leaves
on water.
The wake is breaking into the mute files of these trees.
In the sparse rain,
the glistening macadam extends even the faintest light.

High on the mountain,
one tree stands taller than all the rest.
It leans toward the upward part of the mountain.
Its branches all point upwards.
They grow only on the high side of the tree.
The other side is bare,
its bark struck off by a lightning bolt.
Now it stands, looking brave and terrified.

The mountain is loud with the sounds of dew.
Every rock face weeps teary beads, rivulets
run into beds worn into rock and soil,
between roots, in ditches by the roadways.

I drive higher and feel colder air.
I round a hairpin curve. An elegant buck leaps
so close I hit my brakes hard. His handsome rectangular
hindquarter disappears in the thicket
and then the doe, her fawn behind her,
arches across the road in two bow-shaped leaps
into the woods.
All three disappear into silence.

At the top I stop, drive around the parking lot,
then leap onto a wall
and look into two hundred degrees of blue distance.
A car comes up behind me.
A boy in a wheelchair, a man and a woman get out.
No one speaks.

The mists keep rising from hidden but imaginable valleys.
The mists look like the tops of seas
which are turning gaseous
between the water they rise from
and the air.

Child's Grave, Hale County, Alabama

JIM SIMMERMAN

Someone drove a two-by-four
through the heart of this hard land
that even in a good year
will notch a plow blade worthless,
snap the head off a shovel,
or bow a stubborn back.
He'd have had to steal
the wood from a local mill
or steal, by starlight, across
his landlord's farm, to worry
a fence post out of its well
and lug it the three miles home.
He'd have had to leave his wife
asleep on a corn-shuck mat,
leave his broken brogans
by the stove, to slip outside,
lullaby soft, with the child
bundled in a burlap sack.
What a thing to have to do
on a cold night in December,
1936, alone
but for a raspy wind
and the red, rock-ridden dirt
things come down to in the end.
Whoever it was pounded
this shabby half cross
into the ground must have toiled
all night to root it so:
five feet buried with the child
for the foot of it that shows.
And as there are no words
carved here, it's likely that
the man was illiterate,
or addled with fatigue,
or wrenched simple minded
by the one simple fact.

Or else the unscored lumber
driven deep into the land
and the hump of busted rock
spoke too plainly of his grief—
forty years laid by and still
there are no words for this.

After the Ice

WESLEY MCNAIR

Suddenly, the town
as it was before
the season of ice:

trees, deeper
than anyone
can remember,

ancient farmhouses
resting on stone—
and in the field,

taking the first
sun, two
lost Buicks

standing shoulder
to shoulder, hay
still in their mouths.

Morning

JIM HARRISON

The mirror tastes him
breath clouds
hands pressed against glass

in yellow morning light
a jay
flutters in unaccustomed
silence
from bush to limb of elm

a cow at breakfast
pauses
her jaws lax in momentary stillness

far off a milk truck
rattles
on the section road

light low mist
floats
over the buckwheat
through the orchard

the neighbor's dogs bark
then four roosters announce
day.

on the north porch

SHERYL L. NELMS

twin rinse tubs
steam in the October morning

as Gram poles the clothes
from the Maytag

flops them into the wringer

runs them through
two hot water soaks

the final squeeze
and flapjacks them into
the bushel basket

their cleanness ready
for her red knuckled hanging

on down the line

Deserted Cabin

JOHN HAINES

Here in the yellowing
aspen grove
on Campbell's Hill
the wind is searching
a fallow garden.

I remember the old man
who lived here.
Five years have gone by,
and his house has grown
to resemble his life—
a shallow cave hung
with old hides, rusty
traps and chains,
smelling of eighty years
of unwashed bedding
and rotting harness.

I see him sitting there
now as he used to,
his starved animals gathered
about his bony knees.
He talks to himself
of poverty, cursing softly,
jabbing a stick
at the shadows.

The bitterness of a soul
that wanted only to walk
in the sun and pick
the ripening berries.

It is like coming home
late in the evening
with a candle in your hand,
and meeting someone
you had forgotten—
the voice is strange.

It is the cold autumn wind
stirring the frozen grass,
as if some life
had just passed there,
bound home
in the early darkness.

The Hermitage

BILL DODD

There's an old ranch that's
nothing more than a crumbling adobe
on a high mesa,
framed in wood,
sagging badly.
Despite the sweeping mountain view,
I wonder why built here,
not closer to the river?
With the moon visible this morning,
it seems more planetary than rural,
old, perhaps a hundred years,
and boarded up a quarter century.
The porch was scalloped once,
and there is a red-brick walk,
things suggesting family.

The present heir says the ranch is "working,"
meaning there's someone living
in the nearby trailer,
feeding his wife's horses,
her English riding hobby,
grazing in the yard
where children chased with devil's-claws,
small voices through sage,
a lunar void otherwise.

Seeing Cooch

WESLEY MCNAIR

Most winter days,
passing that
wreck of a house
all wrapped
in plastic,
you do not
find him. It just
sits by the ramp
to 89 like
a great loaf
of bread. Yet
there are times
just before
your mind closes
on the traffic
toward Concord, you see
the slow, black
coat of Cooch.
He will be out
on his failed
porch, studying
a tire or something
without a drawer.

Some nights you see him
in a room beyond
his plastic-covered
windows, moving
in the afterlife
of ruined things.

Home

GEORGE BOGIN

It seemed to me
that the old family house
of my boyhood
was being razed.
The three-story brick front
had been sheared away.
Sunlight glared on the wallpaper.
I saw the living room
and through the French doors
the dining room.
I looked into my room.
No bed. No bookcase. No desk.
Snow began to fall and fall
like tickets
to a million movies.

Mining Town

X. J. KENNEDY

Sheds for machines that lower tons of men
Clasp dirt for dear life. Clapboard houses lose
Gray clapboards the way a dying oak sheds bark.
One house they tell of plunged
Nose-down into a shaft last year with cries
Of people waking, falling.

Like boys in sneakers testing limber ice,
Gas stations growing bold now inch up near.
Who ever thinks that Kitchen Kounter World
Straddles Pit One? Thick coal-oil-colored clouds
Graze to the west.

It takes a while to learn to sleep on edge,
Always on edge, these townsmen like their trees
Locked to the wind's steep angle. When fear tells
It tells out of the corner of an eye,
A rickety house balancing in uncertainty.

Hard

JIM WAYNE MILLER

Hardburly. The name tells how life was here.
I was jerked up, hard, in a deep holler
where smoke from the smoldering gob pile hung in air
that smelled like carbide and warm dishwater.

Hardburly bullies roamed the camp.
Their fists broke my teeth before I worked
clanking shifts of hard coal seams and slabs,
bolting the dripping roof of gray jack rock.

Hard was that roof rock falling when the mine blew,
hard the dying, smothering in the dark.
"This is a real hard thing to have to do,"
the commissioner said, and read our names off a card.

Hard even the Hardburly burial.
They brought us out of darkness into night,
then to the cemetery on this rocky knoll.
They had to dig our graves with dynamite.

Peabody #7 Strip Mine

DAVID BAKER

And that's what they did, strip. Even now,
twenty, forty, eighty years later—
who'll say for sure—the land lies ripped
and scattered like an animal no one
bothered to drag off the road:

its white bones still stick out
from the ground. In the deepest sites
water stands, too, where the cranes wheezed,
and where, before that, a hundred men
broke their backs with shovels

and picks. It was true, though,
if you could just lift a layer off
the earth, you'd have coal, fine, pure
as it came. Now the kids come
to swim the still green pools, and dodge

the balls of cottonmouths that knot
themselves together and sink down,
down. No one's ever bitten.
So out here, mid-dusk, I will stand
and watch something else I have

never understood. Soon it will be night.
And the sky will turn black, blacker
even than the smoke someone dreamed
in that first, good dream
that started all of this.

Bill Spraker's Store, or the Day Geronimo Couldn't Find the Scoop

DAVID HUDDLE

It took some courage just
to walk in there where
it smelled like last year's
potatoes in the cellar,
no windows and only one
45-watt lightbulb,
and Bill'd run you out fast
if you didn't say what you wanted
and pay for it right away.
And after that movie showed
up at the Fries Drive-In,
they started calling Bill
Geronimo because he'd killed
Frenchie Paris one night
with a 20-gauge shotgun,
got acquitted on self-defense
(even though Frenchie
didn't have but one arm),
came home nervous,
with his red hair getting kinkier
and his paleface wife
and daughters getting fatter
and sleepier by the minute,
and Bill had to stop
selling ice cream after they started
spreading that lie around town,
about how Geronimo
couldn't find the scoop one day
and so spit tobacco juice on his hand,
reached in and got a gob
and served up the cone
anyway.

Lil Abner's

PEGGY SHUMAKER

Before they fixed the place up
ropers used to heel each other and
jerk into loose dirt the drunkest
s.o.b.'s in from the ranch.
Naked women never had a chance—
the management tried to keep them,
genuine velvet, over the bar, but one
at least had always to hang
here by the door, so guys could rub her
and get lucky. My dad never roped,
nor rode, nor put down boilermakers
till he couldn't see. Heck,
he just sold Chevies. But he took
us all in on the way to the races,
Tucson Speedway, that halo of hay bales
where stock cars and micro midgets
bar-roomed in our ears
long past the checkered flag.
Yeah, he acted like Hank Arnold #1
who kissed the trophy girls always
whether or not he won. He took us in
like Abner's was a union meeting
and his dues all paid up, took us
and ordered three Cokes with two
cherries each and one Coors draft,
leaned over to elbow the raw jokes
that sent us girls by ourselves
to the john, where it clanged cowbells
and ripped sirens outside
whenever a woman sat down.

Dancing on the Bar at the Blue Goose Saloon

GRACE BAUER

We have stumbled tonight
from bar to bar, settling
here for the pool, the choice
of tunes on the Wurlitzer
that starts on a kick.

The place is packed with cowboys
chasing Jim Beam with Olympia,
complaining about the tourists
they're sick of already,
though happy to drink off their money.

When a local lady says *it's time*
I summon what grace I possess
and follow her lead from bar stool to bar,
managing a precarious cancan
on the beer-slick mahogany.

The obliging bartender clears
our path of mugs and pitchers
with one clean sweep of his arm.
An Indian across the room
curses, chalks his cue
like it's our fault he scratched
on the eight ball.

Outside, a mountain man hangs
bare-assed from a neon fowl,
carrying on about whiskey
and women and howling
at the stark Montana moon.

Everything to Go

ALICE FULTON

It's the Dine-Out Drive-In
where mutant bruiser
trucks gunned by men handcuffed
in tattoos punish the rumble-

strips, and formalin women
on graveyard shifts
feed their kids,
kids, kids.

A tank-topped hitchhiker
jibs, bobs, plays
air guitar nearby.
She primps, applying ptomaine

glares to every snubbing
bumper, and the wide-toothed
comb in her back pocket
marks her as a minor.

"Get in, Fast Food,"
hoots a lead sled of a car.
"I like my ladies cooked
to order and bagged to travel."

"Mister, this ain't Burger King,"
she says. "You don't get it
your way. You take it
my way or you don't get it."

Kids these days, I think.
There's a high-pressure system
over the Midwest
as this clientele that knows

its limits and likes
to exceed them yells
"Everything! To go,"
at loaded intercoms.

"We'll give you a lift
soon as we're finished," I call.
"Yeah, but if some drop-dead
goldcard dude shows first,

I'm a ghost," she says.

In the Amish Bakery

RONALD WALLACE

I don't know why what comes to mind
when I imagine my wife and daughters,
off on a separate vacation
in the family car,
crashing—no survivors—
in one of those Godless snowstorms
of northern Illinois,
is that Amish bakery
in Sauk County, Wisconsin, where,
on Saturday mornings in summer,
we used to go—
all powdered sugar and honey in
the glazed caramel air. And O
the browned loaves rising,
the donuts, buns, and pies, the ripe
strawberry stain of an oven burn
on the cheek of one of the wives.
And outside in the yard
that goddamned trampoline
where we'd imagine them—
the whole blessed family in
their black topcoats and frocks,
their severe hair and beards,

their foolish half-baked grins,
so much flour dust and leaven—
leaping all together on
their stiff sweet legs toward heaven.

Border Café

RUBEN GERARD MARTINEZ

When one enters Nogales, Arizona, and goes into a little
dingy diner which has no utensils or desert pictures,
one finds a disguised threat, which reeks through failing
walls, taming one's appetite limp, and beneath huge sombreros
ragged old men gather outside like a retired gang of banditos.
They piece together their past, sip black-bourbon tea,
and listen to the rain pour near Border Road, the loose gravel
lashing on deportation buses. When one leaves, someone always
closes a curtain, raising a flag like an untucked shirt
blowing in the wind south of the border.

At the Blue Diner

CHRISTINE E. HEMP

A tiny line of moisture traced his lip.
I thought his profile like a boy's
but for the shadow of a beard.
He wore an earring and a ponytail.

Slim hips, apron-tied waist: he wouldn't know
the lines of beauty there,
all his attention on the grill,
dunking fries, flipping beef.

Did he sleep alone?
Did his arm fall loose across his pillow?
Did he whisper in his dreams?

I ate my turkey and potatoes
wondering these things.

Then I caught his eye and said
how good the turkey was.
He smiled and blinked.

But it needs more gravy
I said—would that be okay?

Without a word he turned
and ladled me a steamy cupful.
He slid his finger up the side
to catch the drip and wiped it.

Then with all the grace of one who's
used to giving things away,
he set the cup before me.

Eldora in July

TOM CLARK

a valley
of aspens
and wild flowers

with the wind
dithering in them

In South Dakota There Is a Word

SHERYL NOETHE

In South Dakota there is a word for Hail. The white
combine that drives in the dark and goes against

Nature. "Eight hundred acres," you say over the phone,
"It's like all my friends are waving good-bye from a boat."

"I'm standing onshore waving my ticket. This is the
year I was supposed to make it. Instead I crawled beneath

my tractor and watched the hail take my crop."

When the stalks are damaged the heads of the sunflowers
keep filling while their own weight wrestles them down

to the ground. You watch for slow weeks and when all
their faces are in the mud you decide to go into town.

The sky froze and turned white and cracked and fell down.

25

High Plains Rag

JAMES GALVIN

But like remorse
the prairie grass
seeks emptiness,

increases
in its sleep,
gets even

with the fragrant,
stoic sage.
Oh it is witless

and blind.
It cannot remember
what it was doing

with all that wind.
It waits
for a thimbleful of rain.

It populates such distances
it must be brave
but prairie grass

bends down in sorrow
to be so lost,
and like remorse,

feels
so nearly endless
it cannot ever stop.

Lilies

W. R. MOSES

In a strip of old prairie, paradoxically spared
For lying close beside a destructive agent
Of prairies, a railway, I remember one could in season
Go hunting lilies. Of course not the overscented,
Undercolored domestic lilies that speak
From funeral houses and altars of death and resurrection.
Rather, wild tiger lilies, low-scented, high-colored,
With petals recurved like snarls, black-spotted on orange.
One time I saw them leaning over the bones
Of (possibly) a prairie chicken caught on her nest by fire.
They seemed a right tribute to honor a wild death.
As for resurrection—they nodded in the prairie wind.

Landscape: near Moab, Utah

JONATHAN HOLDEN

All morning, drifting among the tall
volumes of that rock library
we kept our voices hushed, as if those rocks—
great wrinkled scholars hunched against the sky—
were frowning over matters far
more momentous than we were
while our voices, lightweight, silly
as the voices of schoolchildren
in such a company of elders, floated
about their shoulders, rolled off their backs.
Some landscapes invite us to fall in love
with them. Their features,
like the countenances of the very beautiful,
remain ambiguous, composite of so many
slowly dissolving human expressions
that, like the faces of the famous,

they promise intimacy with everyone
at once. Though they be eyeless,
though they hold their pose, perfectly demure,
it's as if the gaze of a shadow or a tree,
the empty gaze of even light itself
held some indication, could answer us.
Whichever way we turn, they turn
with us slightly. We stop. They stop,
waiting for us. Nothing moves.
Like beautiful women, the rocks return
our gaze, expectant. There is no need for speech.
Their gaze means everything at once.

Pecos Valley Poem

KEITH WILSON

It was a different world then,
I tell my children, as men have
always done. There were two hotels
—The Commercial and the Rio Pecos—
over there. Your great-grandfather
carried people and baggage in his wagon
from the train station down there
up to the hotels and the people
were fed and given rooms and in
the evenings used to sit out on
big porches and stare at customers
of the other hotel next door.

Or maybe they'd walk down to
the drugstore and have a Coke
or walk across the street and look
into the window of the dry goods
store or the grocery. It was really
quiet at night. You can't imagine
how still everything became. Lights
out at seven for most people, not

much electricity in the homes, no
body on the road that led off across
the mesa to magical places with
unfamiliar names.

           One evening
a bunch of people were listening
to election results on the drug
store's radio and two headlights
like puma eyes appeared out of
the Llano's darkness and one man said,
"Now would you just look at that!
Some damn fool out there on the road,
and after dark, too!" That's the way
it was in those small villages
along the glittering Pecos, those days.

Rough Country

DANA GIOIA

Give me a landscape made of obstacles,
of steep hills and jutting glacial rock,
where the low-running streams are quick to flood
the grassy fields and bottomlands.
                A place
no engineers can master—where the roads
must twist like tendrils up the mountainside
on narrow cliffs where boulders block the way.

Where tall black trunks of lightning-scalded pine
push through the tangled woods to make a roost
for hawks and swarming crows.
                And sharp inclines
where twisting through the thorn-thick underbrush,
scratched and exhausted, one turns suddenly

to find an unexpected waterfall,
not half a mile from the nearest road,
a spot so hard to reach that no one comes—

a hiding place, a shrine for dragonflies
and nesting jays, a sign that there is still
one piece of property that won't be owned.

Cannon Hill

SANDRA HOCHMAN

A farm. A cannon on a hill.
Long ago I sat beneath that cannon
And picked clover. Often, at sunset,
I walked down to the barn, and held my arm
Around a calf, or took the one-eyed pony for a ride.
Later, I walked in the forests of corn.
The stalks were palm boughs, strands of yellow sun.
Evenings, I picked tomato vines.
Earth clung to them, they prickled in my hand.
And our house was always lit. My grandfather
Furnished it from his Broadway Theatrical Warehouse.
Everything only seemed to be what it was: cupboards
Didn't open, prop tables had three sides,
Books were cardboard thick, lamps dimmed on,
Statuettes were paper silhouettes—
Papier-mâché, they seemed to have no weight upon the farm.
Even the cannon had come home
From a play about war. It had been in
A smash hit in which Nazis, like
Chippewas, lost. There it stood,
Up on our hill, made out of wood,
Soggy and warping from the summer rain.

Cannon Hill Farm was sold. Black
Out. Nothing works but a kitchen knife.

The Barn

MARY OLIVER

We sold the goats,
We gave the chickens away,
We buried Grandfather.
Now there's this hulk on the hill

Big as a ship and its beams cracking,
Growing shabby with litter and storage,
Growing cold as a corpse.
I stand under the webby rafters

Wondering what comes next,
Wanting flood or fire, some ceremony
Final as the hole in the ground
That hid Grandfather

When he was done being busy,
Done pitching hay,
Clanging the milk pails,
Tending his bearded ladies.

Outside, on the cooling hills,
I watch the leaves swirl down.
The year, like an old king,
Knows that its story is over

And dies commanding all
Its signs to follow,
Leaves nothing for time to diminish.
We could learn a lesson

But won't; with frost in the air,
We mend the broken window,
We lock the door, and huddle
From erosion everywhere.

Small Farms Disappearing in Tennessee

—Newspaper Headline

JIM WAYNE MILLER

Sometimes a whole farm family comes awake
in a close dark place over a motor's hum
to find their farm's been rolled up like a rug
with them inside it. They will be shaken onto
the streets of Cincinnati, Dayton or Detroit.

It's a ring, a syndicate dismantling farms
on dark nights, filing their serial numbers
smooth, smuggling them north like stolen cars,
disposing of them part by stolen part.

Parts of farms turn up in unlikely places:
weathered gray boards from a Tennessee burley tobacco
barn are up against the wall of an Ohio
office building, lending a rustic effect.
A Tennessee country church suddenly appeared
disguised as a storefront in Uptown Chicago.
Traces of Tennessee farms are found on the slopes
of songs written in Bakersfield, California.
One missing farm was found intact at the head
of a falling creek in a recently published short story.
One farm that disappeared without a clue
has turned up in the colorful folk expressions
of a state university buildings and grounds custodian.
A whole farm was found in the face of Miss Hattie Johnson,
lodged in a Michigan convalescent home.

Soil samples taken from the fingernails
of Ford plant workers in a subdivision
near Nashville match those of several farms
which recently disappeared in the eastern end of the state.
A seventy-acre farm that came to light
in the dream of a graduate student taking part
in a Chicago-based dream research project
has been put on micro-cards for safe keeping.

33

Divers searching for a stolen car
on the floor of an Army Corps of Engineers'
impoundment discovered a roadbed, a silo, a watering
trough and the foundations of a dairy barn.
Efforts to raise the farm proved unsuccessful.
A number of small Tennessee farms were traced
to a land developer's safe-deposit box
in a midstate bank after a bank official
entered the vault to investigate roosters
crowing and cows bawling inside the box.

The Agricultural Agency of the state
recently procured a helicopter to aid
in the disappearing farm phenomenon.
"People come in here every week," the Agency head,
Claude Bullock, reports, "whole families on tractors,
claiming their small farm has disappeared."
Running the Small Farms arm of the Agency
is not just a job for Bullock, born and brought up
on a small Tennessee farm himself. "We're doing
the best we can," says Bullock, a soft-spoken man
with a brow that furrows like a well-plowed field
over blue eyes looking at you like farm ponds.
"But nowadays," he adds, "you can punch a farm,
especially these small ones, onto computer cards.
You can store them away on magnetic tapes.
So they're hard to locate with a helicopter."

Bullock's own small farm, a thirty-acre
remnant of "the old home place," disappeared
fourteen months ago, shortly before
he joined the Small Farms arm of the Agency.

Chicken Coop Hill

THOM TAMMARO

The hill is not
far from town,
just above Summit Avenue
behind Gull's Run.

I was told the same story:
that years back
the hill was used by
white-hooded Klansmen
to burn their crosses
on summer nights.

At midnight
they would gather
at the bottom of the hill
and begin their procession
in white, crosses held high
above their heads,
to the top of the hill
chanting some devil's prayer.

And when they reached the top
would scatter their flaming
crosses across the crest
of the hill

drive the burning stakes
in the heart of
Chicken Coop Hill,
blood flames raging
for the whole town to see.

There are no more burnings.
No more marches in symbolic robes.

Even the wire coops
have long been emptied
of screaming white chickens
kicking around dust.

Half the hill
has been pressed over
with red bricks, made a road,
houses lining each side.

Now where the road ends
Chicken Coop Hill begins.

Yet I remember
how some of us would gather
at the bottom of the hill
and hike to the top,
now covered with trail bike
and rabbit tracks,

and after spending long
summer afternoons up there
among rusted wire coops and
damp wood spread with moss,
would drag our ragged bodies
down the hill

and heat waves
would rise like liquid ghosts
from the hot bricks.

In the Orchard

R. T. SMITH

Between the back door and the uphill
springhouse, I watch the season wheel
through the orchard where sour apples
drop sapless to the grass and the trellis
collapses with its weight of broken
wood, but no grapes. Queen Anne's
lace withers and star-grass petals drift.
When I look up, the maples are flaming
like stories from the Bible, sycamores
shine like fool's gold, but then
the sweet stench of a rotting possum
snags all attention near the steep bank
of goldenrod. In bramble by the last
bearing spartan branch, hornets orbit
their nest lazily, as if unaware of winter
edging south over the mountains.
From the springhouse roof I can see far
into the next county where gypsy moths
quietly strangle the saplings. Brisk change
rides the air as blood accelerates
to warm my nerves, and I survey
this brief demesne, wild to discover
the source of sorrow surely impending,
the source of this cold nameless joy.

blues on the ranch

JACK ANDERSON

We spend our evenings on the ranch
listening to our denims fade,
hearing the throb of blue threads turning white
and the soft twangings as the knees wear away.

You can't see them change, it's like watching a clock:
you look and you look and nothing has happened,
then, after you do something, when you look again
there's a place worn right through and another one starting.

But in the evening when the sun goes down
the denim starts chanting of its day of hard labor
while the rivets tap like little castanets—
O hear your jeans singing, drunk on your sweat.

They know nothing but you, they hug you, their hero.
O hear your jeans fading as they live out your life.

Cousin Ella Goes to Texas

GEORGE ELLA LYON

I reckon it was 19 and 52
and I was gonna drive Bea and her kids
to Corpus Christi Texas in my old Chev
and my brother Joe took a look at her and said
Eller, you gonna slide right into Mexico on them tires.
So I went up to Frank Gergley's and said, Frank
I'm fixin to take Bea and her two out to Texas
and I need new tires. I didn't have much money
but he said Time would be fine.
Got his boy Oxie to unlug the old tires
then wrenched the new ones on hisself.
They weren't brand-new, but they had grit.

So I drove her home and we loaded her
and before the sun could slip its egg in the pan next mornin
we was off. Bea's two, Rhonda and Mark,
didn't even get carsick till we hit the Smokies.
Well, we'd got the kids cleaned off
and were bearin down on Memphis
and Bea'd broke out the bologna sandwiches
when I heard it
first like a beaver slappin his tail:
k-thwack, k-thwunk, k-thwack, k-thwunk.
What's that? Bea had a bite balled up
in the side of her mouth like a squirrel.
Well, it ain't the song of the open road, I told her.
I guess we better pull over and have her checked.

Man came out grinnin. I said
I got somethin wrong with my tires. You check
the back ones after you fill her up. And he did.
Bea and the kids were huntin the Ladies
when he slunk around the side of the car.

Looks like your retreads is comin loose, mayam,
he said, pourin it out like syrup. I like to knocked
his pitcher over gettin out of that car.
What do you mean retreads? These is brand-new
secondhand tires. No mayam, they's retreads
and the new tread's about to let go.

I could've boiled over like a radiator, I was
that mad—at Frank and Bea and Texas and them tires
and dollars for not growin nowheres that you can get to—
but I just said Shoot and kicked one up front.
Only one in the bunch that kept its scalp.

Horseshoes. Marfa, Texas.

MICHAEL PETTIT

Connect, connect. It's a refrain
I don't call out
or question. What and who
would I ask? The two old men
in straw hats and overalls
who walk from stake to stake
without a word to each other?
I watch summer dusk lift
the pecan trees of Marfa,
barren this year, into relief,
into the sky a blue
I'll call Mediterranean.
I lean against a trunk, suddenly
some Roman soldier under the leathery
lance-shaped leaves of an olive.
Wind off the sea rattling
through the leaves and my hair,
I never look up. I start pitching
my mule's lost shoe over
and over at a sharp white rock
as I wait for the afternoon
to blow away. It does.

Wind and the light move
over land and water, touching
who knows who. I don't. Marfa
is nowhere and what I have
are these two, absorbed
with the swing of their arms
and the flight of the shoe end
over end or in a slow flat spin.
Light gone, their eyes pinched
like mine in the dark
of these towering, still pecans,
I know they listen, hoping
for the familiar quick ring
of iron on iron
as their shoe strikes the stake
and they see the brief
true spark fly.

Going for Peaches, Fredericksburg, Texas

NAOMI SHIHAB NYE

Those with experience look for a special kind.
Red Globe, the skin slips off like a fine silk camisole.
Boy breaks one open with his hands. Yes it's good,
my old relatives say, but we'll look around.
They want me to stop at every peach stand
between Stonewall and Fredericksburg,
leave the air conditioner running,
jump out and ask the price.

Coming up here they talked about
the best ways to die. One favors a plane crash,
but not over a city. One wants to make sure
her grass is watered when she goes.
Ladies, ladies! This peach is fine,
it blushes on both sides.
But they want to keep driving.

In Fredericksburg the houses are stone,
they remind me of wristwatches, glass polished,
years ticking by in each wall.
I don't like stone, says one. What if it fell?
I don't like Fredericksburg, says the other.
Too many Germans driving too slow.
She herself is German as Stuttgart.
The day presses forward, wearing complaints
like charms on its bony wrist.

Actually ladies (I can't resist),
I don't think you wanted peaches after all,
you just wanted a nip of scenery,
some hills to tuck behind your heads.
The buying starts immediately, from a scarfed woman
who says she gave up teachin' for peachin'.
She has us sign a guest book.
One aunt insists on reloading into her box
to see the fruit on the bottom.
One rejects any slight bruise.
But ma'am, the seller insists, nature isn't perfect.
Her hands are spotted, like a peach.

On the road, cars weave loose patterns between lanes.
We will float in flowery peach-smell
back to our separate kettles, our private tables
and knives, and line up the bounty,
deciding which ones go where.
A canned peach, says one aunt, lasts ten years.
She was 87 last week. But a frozen peach
tastes better on ice cream.
Everything we have learned so far,
skins alive and ripening, on a day
that was real to us, that was summer,
motion going out and memory coming in.

Kitchen Window

R. T. SMITH

The western distances, so many exquisite
brush strokes, try to come closer—tree
line, fields, fencerow with its persimmon
shrubs, the lake and its white jade
shimmer, the lawn. I can't focus
on the red clay road or a cluster of black
cattle grazing. Venus is just beginning
to show, and one cloud alters, darkens,
threatens rain onto all this dust,
which frets my vision even more and is
everywhere, like loneliness, like a longing
for cool sleep or heaven. I stand
at the sink, my hands cool
in rusty water, eyes filling
with distance approaching. A flaw
in the air promises weather, and just
past the ragweed and sheep sorrel, the charred
silhouette of a white oak
struck last August by lightning
stretches its gnarled arms and hopes
for thrown fire, one more chance to writhe
and blaze like an angel.

Bare Yard

ROBERT MORGAN

My grandma swept her yard
often as the floor
and wore out willow switches
and swatches of broom sedge
sewn in bundles
to whisk away the twigs
and pebbles, leaves and chicken piles.
She washed down the soiled places
with buckets from the spring
and sprinkled branch sand
over any chicken tracks or stains
that might show through,
and brushed it clean as snow.
How fresh the yard looked then.
You didn't want to track
the virgin cover so white,
so perfect a sheet sparkling
with quartz and mica, and kept
to the edges of the boxwoods.
The yard was isled with tufts
of grass near its borders.
Grandma placed her geraniums out there
in their brick-clay pots.
The ground looked plain and hard
as her expression while she worked.
Cropped grass was for the pasture
and graveyard and meadow.
She set a few gourds and unusual
rocks by the steps and flower beds.
Otherwise the space was bare and bright
in the sun as her conscience.

An English Garden in Autumn

CHRISTINE E. HEMP

The garden is empty under naked trees
And not a breeze cares to pass or settle in
Or breathe a sigh in order to release
Two leaves from their tableau upon the thin
Arms of plum and maple poised for winter frieze.

On the Back Porch

DORIANNE LAUX

The cat calls for her dinner.
On the porch I bend and pour
brown soy stars into her bowl,
stroke her dark fur.
It's not quite night.
Pinpricks of light in the eastern sky.
Above me my neighbor's roof, a transparent
moon, a pink rag of cloud.
Inside my house are those who love me.
My daughter dusts biscuit dough.
And there's a man who will lift my hair
in his hands, brush it
until it throws sparks.
Everything is just as I've left it.
Dinner simmers on the stove.
Glass bowls wait to be filled
with gold broth. Sprigs of parsley
on the cutting board.
I want to smell this rich soup, the air
around me going dark, as stars press
their simple shapes into the sky.
I want to stay on the back porch
while the world tilts
toward sleep, until what I love
misses me, and calls me in.

In the Garage

JULIE MARTIN

There is someone in our garage.
We've lived here seven years
and never guessed he was there.
But finding out today, I nodded,
somehow knowing all along,
by the way the windows
glower in the evening,
and by the low gasp I hear
when I open the door too fast,
and by the way the whole building
is hunkered down there under the trees,
shifting its weight,
back on its haunches.

He must think he's in his own barn.
But that was torn down years ago,
and this wide hulking garage
built on the same spot,
out of the same lumber,
I suspect.
He doesn't even know
that his house is all changed,
and that the streets
are paved all over town,
and that the high pine grove
by the river
is gone to a gravel pit.
He's in there,
maybe thinking he's safe,
or maybe not thinking at all,
just waiting
in our garage,
damp at night
and dusty during the day.

I don't think we've ever
parked a car in there,
and no matter how many times
we clear out the stuff to make
a workshop or potting table
—things close in again—
especially that back corner
where the junk is piled
halfway to the rafters,
nearly to where his feet must be
as he hangs,
turning slowly
with the draft
under the door.

The Closet

BROOKE HORVATH

I

The closet rests in a dream of cedar, of clothes
waiting to walk through rooms of blinding sunlight
of which the closet has heard vague rumors.

Although the closet owns a dozen pairs of shoes or more,
like a small child it cannot tie one shoelace,
like a child it longs to run away to sea and change its name.

Wishing to be left alone with its sweaters and golf clubs,
the closet, affectedly signing itself "Clothespress," knows
it has no life of its own, is loved only for its possessions.

In a camphor dialogue with darkness, the closet masquerades as the space
beneath the bed, the cupboard in which the dead child's toys are kept,
knowing itself neither a symbol nor a metaphor.

II

The closet imagines it has sold its memoirs to Hollywood.
Robert Redford will star in a Dennis Hopper film
based on the closet's addiction to soiled linen.

Fancying itself a rising star, wishing to be called Cubby,
the closet demands a new wardrobe, better lighting,
covering its walls with pinups of guest rooms of the rich and famous.

Dreams of success lie piled to the closet's ceiling.
It posts new rules: storage of paint thinner or insecticides prohibited!
No clandestine sex during parties! No walking in unannounced!

Every week cheap tabloids will lie about the closet's contents,
gossip columnists ask, "What will the closet hold next?"
The closet will install a pool, be seen in all the right homes.

III

Such adolescent dreams the closet once entertained:
of padded, scented hangers, ample, well-ordered shelves,
tidy rows of pastel frocks with labels reading "Dry Clean Only."

Meanwhile, the closet has been forced to take a second job.
Working weekends and evenings as a longshoreman,
the closet begins making off-color remarks about armoires.

The closet feels unfulfilled, seeks excitement in danger,
suggests itself as the perfect place to stash pharmaceuticals.
Here, it whispers, behind the quilts, underneath the mukluks.

Having lost its morals, its sense of right and wrong, the closet
now packs a rod, obscene underwear from mail-order catalogs.
Guests turn away embarrassed from life-size dolls behind the tennis dresses.

IV

The closet cannot sleep, it's so upset. No one
looks anymore for his old mitt or her old muff.
No one cares any longer about the secret life of storage space.

The closet feigns indifference—its comforting darkness
becomes a refuge in which it fumes and fusses, grumbling
about moths and other things over which it has no control.

Why is there so much dust? the closet queries. How long must I entertain
wet umbrellas, boorish boots? Have I lost my youthful vim?
The closet fears it has become a metaphor.

This fear proves stifling. The closet may as well be nailed shut,
a locker for bafflement, a cabinet for silence and stale air.
The closet wishes it had never been built.

Something Smaller

JIM HALL

Because they are moving into something smaller
the Weed Eater must go, the power tools,
the four-poster, my mother's mother's desk,
my father's father's tackle box.
Books flaky as last season's maple leaves.
I'm here to haul it all away
because I have room now, growing.
Their new apartment, the downward curve,
hasn't many closets. They're through
storing anyway, ready to give up, admit
they'll never get around to using this and that.
And they want to pass on what they can
while everyone is healthy.
We are in the double garage, and it is,
can you use this? how about this?
Probably, yes. Probably I can.
But what I truly want would take a fleet
of trucks to haul away. I want the years-ago
house, its orchard and fish pond, its rotting
carriage house, the wild raspberries behind it,
mud daubers in its rafters. The smokehouse.
The dogwoods, mimosa, pear and peach.
I want the lawn I raked and mowed and lay in.

I want the endless jobs, always just staying even.
I want my parents there, stacking hatboxes
in the closets, filling the basement with albums
and mannequins and Victrolas and Kentucky rifles.
I want the house to grow too small, and for them
to talk of moving to something with a barn.
I want the countryside. Simple green hills and
sugar maples and cows and wood smoke and
curvy roads that ran off to the lake
or to the city. But it is the Weed Eater
I will unload, far off. I need one.
The weeds where I live now are vicious
and unremitting.

Moving

JIM HEYNEN

Groping toward departure, we are
shedding more than old skin, more
than we started with. Here
is yet another
empty box. How shall we fill it?
Can we really
contain ourselves again, drift
off with the inconstant clouds,
emptying ourselves as we go?
And what can I say to you? I
love you. I love
what has grown here, our
daughter swimming
past windows, rising
beyond us. We grow small.
Great sky, will you remember our short passage?
Little house, little bed, little chair,
will you believe us again?
Here, earth, take what we have lost.
Here, wind, deliver this promise to a friend.

Now, wheels, roll us home,
wherever home begins. Give us
a good journey
and a safe forgetting.

Closing the House

JIM WAYNE MILLER

While rumbling trunks pushed down the hall upstairs
boom like the scudding thunderstorm just passed,
we bear out cardboard boxes, tables, and chairs
stripped from rooms grown hollow, strange and vast.
We plod, as humdrum over such a deep
as veteran thieves lifting petty loot,
too dried-sweat stiff to feel the sweep
of grief that rolls the floor from underfoot.
Mule-footed plundering done, the rooms all sacked,
now only the furrowed shell that stops the door
remains, impounding the roaring foaming fact
all the years. I pick it off the floor.
It murmurs in my ear, floods my breath,
and drowns me in the sea-sound of your death.

Ware's Cove

GAIL MAZUR

Odd, to find the little square snapshot caught
in the back of a dresser drawer:
my grandfather (I'd been thinking of him)

dwarfed in an Adirondack chair on the dock.
My father would have set him up there,
holding a bamboo fishing pole,

and had the old black Kodak ready.
It would have been a Sunday during the War.
Across the river, feverish woods

and the changing house aren't in the picture.
Nor kids, screaming and splashing
while a lifeguard dozes on his tower.

Once, when the cove was dammed,
the whole neighborhood came down
to rake the riverbed which was mined

with broken bottles. My brother's feet
and mine still bear the moon-shaped scars.
Later, a girl drowned there.

At night, I'd picture the disconnected
body, memorizing Red Cross rescues
that would never beat the river's current.

Now there's no one I love
to say what fish Grandfather caught
in the not-yet-polluted water,

and no one—not anyone living
in the identical stupid houses
squeezed side to vinyl side

where the innocent woods once were—
no one can have swum here since.
There is no blue-lipped boy,

skinny and shivering, no hopeful girl,
no vigilant mother with Noxzema
and towels and tears, calling her in.

Sundown on Glimpse Lake

CHARLES HARPER WEBB

Wind drops
like a negligee
to the forest
floor. Dusk
steps out, warm,
pine-scented.

Whitecaps
on the lake
melt down
to ripples,
then to smooth
gray glass.

Red sunlight
spears
our startled
eyes, then
slips behind
green mountains

as the moon
slowly
crawls out of
its dark
cave
in the sky.

Biloxi Beach Drama

ROSALIE BURKES DANIELS

The moon,
silver tomcat,
struts across the still night—
the waves, disturbed, throw nightcaps
at him.

Devil's Finger Island

PAUL RUFFIN

A finger rises
from the sea here,
with shells and spines
and sea-worn wood
clotted in sand:
rises from the
dark palm of the sea
to lodge bright as a beam
in the corner of God's blue eye.

A Grammar of the Sea

RICHARD SNYDER

The absolute and plural possessive sea
asserts itself, is its own subject; strand
is modifier. Water takes the land
as its direct object; regularly
it sends its finite action and *to be*
against the passive, paraphrastic sand
which translates green syntax into white band,
thus parsing such compound complexity.

But antecedent sea stays its green self,
unclassifiable and unabridged,
its manner, arrangement, choice and style bars
to analysis. It sends toward land's shelf
shrugging shoulders, then sighs out. Privileged
in rhetoric, it richly rolls its R's.

Journeyman's Wages

CLEMENS STARCK

To the waters of the Willamette I come
in nearly perfect weather,
Monday morning
traffic backed up at the bridge
a bad sign.
                    Be on the job at eight,
boots crunching in gravel;
cinch up the tool belt, string out the cords
to where we left off on Friday—
that stack of old
form lumber, that bucket of rusty bolts
and those two beat-up sawhorses
wait patiently for us.

Gil is still drunk, red-eyed, pretending he's not
and threatening to quit;
Gordon is studying the prints.
Slab on grade, tilt-up panels, Glu-lams
and trusses . . .

Boys, I've got an idea—
instead of a supermarket
why couldn't this be a cathedral?

At the Office Early

TED KOOSER

Rain has beaded the panes
of my office windows,
and in each little lens
the bank at the corner
hangs upside down.
What wonderful music
this rain must have made
in the night, a thousand banks
turned over, the change
crashing out of the drawers
and bouncing upstairs
to the roof, the soft
percussion of ferns
dropping out of their pots,
the ballpoint pens
popping out of their sockets
in a fluffy snow
of deposit slips.
Now all day long,
as the sun dries the glass,
I'll hear the soft piano
of banks righting themselves,
the underpaid tellers
counting their nickels and dimes.

The Powerhouse

KEITH WILSON

My dad worked there, part-time, knew about
as much as any of the other guys, excepting always
Smokey Lewis, who ran it, nursed it and cursed it,
keeping the big generators whining and rumbling
from about five o'clock in the afternoon
until about eight in the darkening evening.

I used to sit on the floor of our kitchen
and watch the bare bulb where it hung from the
porcelain insulator on two cloth-insulated wires,
saw it begin to glow just after I heard the voice
of the powerhouse begin to sound from across the
village, near the river. When the bulb was firmly
alight, I relaxed my vigil and went to help Mother
set the table for evening meal, thinking of Father
down there
               where, according to his stories, great
balls of static electricity sometimes rolled across
the floor like Taos witches, but could pass right
through a man's legs without harming him. Or how,
one stormy night, there was a short in the cables that
led through a cement tunnel to the main transformer,
and how he had crawled into the tunnel, just to see
what the hell was happening, maybe where the short
was and got fired out of that tunnel like a big
bag of cloth and bones and if it hadn't been for
Smokey, who knew some artificial respiration, he'd
have been deader than any doornail.

To me, the voice of the powerhouse sounded like a
great wolf, baying over the houses and the people.
I was fascinated by it, but always its presence
touched me with vague fear—fewer and fewer coal
oil lamps glowed in the evenings, the noise grew
and electric bulbs watched out of more and more
windows, their eyes steady and purposeful through
the dark of a winter night beside the Llano.

The Public Library as an Erotic Oasis

GRACE BAUER

Yes, ma'am, *Consumer Reports* says
Westinghouse will keep you warm.

No sir, I do not know
the daily caloric intake of Argentina

and cannot find the name
of Miss Universe for 1963

in *Facts on File*, the *World Almanac*,
not even the *Reader's Guide*; and

I need to get the guard to get
the Peeping Tom to take a walk;

and I've got three boys tittering
over the bra ads in *Vogue*, while

their friends are trying to decide
whether or not to blow their allowances

on microfiche copies of a *Playboy* centerfold,
which is, unfortunately, sliced into

three separate frames, and at a quarter a shot
they're not sure they'll have enough change

left for the streetcar. All the girls
from Sacred Heart are looking for reviews

of *Romeo and Juliet* or *A Tale of Two Cities*.
And me, I just wish they would all go away

so I could sit and stare over the downstairs stacks
or last week's *New York Times*, and dream

about the smell of my lover's hair and the sweet
slippery heat of his tongue.

Zodiac

RON IKAN

Here at work
I share a windowless
room with others
and in my individual corner I have pictures
taped to both walls,

pictures of Arturo Toscanini
and Coleman Hawkins and
an aerial view of Comiskey
Park, Monument Valley in Arizona
and Notre Dame Cathedral, van
Gogh's Starry Night and Stonehenge
and Willie Mays, a freeway

hunkered down somewhere between Cardiff by the Sea and Sagittarius the Archer
which as many cars as there are stars over Southern

California

have traveled on, and on
across the room
to gunmetal desks and green leatherette chairs
arranged in the abstract, one

desk with an apple on it so red it looks purple, another
sporting a photograph of a woman not unlike

a Modigliani, and on out the door
into the parking lot

where slant afternoon weather
tends toward gray and bleak and raw
and the sun goes down at five

o'clock come wintertime, where once last July
a cosmologist in his magenta roadster
sat listening to the Fantasia on a Theme by Thomas Tallis,
contemplating the face of God.

Turn Your Radio On

JIM WAYNE MILLER

I

He couldn't hear his own thoughts in the city that never slept.
Like a voice on a far-off radio station, his thoughts rose
and fell in a storm of static. The city's rush and roar
even poured through his dreams, boiling up like a waterfall.

Asleep or waking, he tried to keep a sense of direction south.
Lying awake in the smoky carbon darkness of northern nights,
facing east, he kept a knowledge, like a book under his pillow,
that the mountains lay to his right, beyond the mills and warehouses.

But sometimes he'd come awake in darkness and find the room
had turned in the slow current of his sleep. He would not rest
again until he'd righted the room, and sleep was drifting
away from the waterfall's roar toward the quietness of mountains.

But he never drifted home before he woke. He felt so stilled
inside, a breathing silence. It was as if his thoughts had been
a friend, a buddy who went everywhere with him. Now he
turned and found that old companion hadn't followed him here.

II

Sometimes he'd sit for hours looking through a shoe box
of family photographs: his grandfather leading a pair of Walker
foxhounds; the old man atop a boulder in the Bearwallow
holding his squirrel gun like a walking stick, or on the porch

with his grandmother, both of them sitting in split-bottom chairs.
Weathered and homemade like the chairs they sat in, and like the house
and barn, so comfortably in place, they looked like one another.
Something about the way they sat spoke to him through his own thoughts

all the way from the mountains, like a powerful transmitter: this place
belongs to us, their faces said, and we belong to it.
When it's time, we come out on this porch and take our ease,
and talk, as naturally as tree frogs in the poplars sing toward dark.

Going North

for my grandfather

LUIS OMAR SALINAS

Those streets in my youth,
hilarious and angry,
cobblestoned by mestizos,
fresh fruit
and dancing beggars.
Gone are the soldiers
and the nuns.
My Portuguese friends
have gone North.
The schoolgirls
have ripened
overnight.
I hum Spanish tunes
waiting for the bus
in Fresno.
These avenues
I watch carefree
young, open collared
like my grandfather
who died in a dream
going North.

The Caboose Factory

RONALD KOERTGE

10,000 men
on the
pasadena
freeway
all in
love
with
the
word
        drifter

Passing Thru

GEOF HEWITT

You see them at truck stops, signs that litter the walls,
Work fascinates me I can sit & watch it for hours, Plan Ahea
And the waitress so sullen you want to tip extra just to show her
How wrong she was about you, her white dress with little bumps
All over the material making it look almost gray and you see thru
To the bra doing its thin job and she wants you to pay up
So she can go home, saunters over and yawns between chews "Youthru?"
And not to be mean but because you're lonely you ask for another donut:
She extends it with aluminum pincers so it seems germproof
But you watched earlier when she emptied the bakery cellophane damn near
Fondling each one as if here at least was something she cared for
And licking all the extra sugar off her fingers at the end.

"To hell with aluminum—let's dance!" you cry and twist her hand
Over the counter so she drops pincers and your donut
"Hey cut that out—whatsa matter with you you crazy or somethin: Joe!"
And she starts yelling but you've already passed thru
That critical tunnel where you decide:
"This is a dream, I'll do what I please"

And one of the truckers looks up from the coffee he stirred with his eyes
As you think of your mother who told you about them and how one
     would kill you someday just like they got your father

And you dance with her back and forth over the countertop
Until Joe comes out at which point the trucker gets involved too
And both of them have you by the legs and the waitress is saying
"Wise guy wise guy" over and over
And the donut and the pincers are on the floor
And if you wanna know more go do it yourself

Switchyard

JOHN WITTE

I'm awake again with the sweet singing
in my ears. Another world
must begin at the end of our road,
the empty boxcars coupling and uncoupling,
their steel wheels ringing where they squeeze the track.

I can hear my sister.
From the woods behind our house,
where I am listening with the turtle
and the brown bird, I think she is raising the flute to her lips.
She's trying for the high, clear notes.

And I can hear in the harbor
the boats coming home loaded with mackerel,
with panic. The fisherman is tired of his work, all day
reaching into the water. I can hear the winches squeal, lifting
the big bucket up out of the hold.

I'm lying perfectly still in the dark,
still awake, still in love with you. If I rise,
and dress, and leave in the direction of these sounds,
I'll come to the tracks, the locomotive moving this way
and that, selecting cars like words in a sentence. I'll find
the stunned angels under the trestle,
stumbling on the cinders.

When they ask for a little change,
I'll be ready. I'll have my whole life there with me.
I'll give it to them.

Filling Station

ELIZABETH BISHOP

Oh, but it is dirty!
—this little filling station,
oil-soaked, oil-permeated
to a disturbing, over-all
black translucency.
Be careful with that match!

Father wears a dirty,
oil-soaked monkey suit
that cuts him under the arms,
and several quick and saucy
and greasy sons assist him
(it's a family filling station),
all quite thoroughly dirty.

Do they live in the station?
It has a cement porch
behind the pumps, and on it
a set of crushed and grease-
impregnated wickerwork;
on the wicker sofa
a dirty dog, quite comfy.

Some comic books provide
the only note of color—
of certain color. They lie
upon a big dim doily
draping a taboret
(part of the set), beside
a big hirsute begonia.

Why the extraneous plant?
Why the taboret?
Why, oh why, the doily?
(Embroidered in daisy stitch
with marguerites, I think,
and heavy with gray crochet.)

Somebody embroidered the doily.
Somebody waters the plant,
or oils it, maybe. Somebody
arranges the rows of cans
so that they softly say:
ESSO—SO—SO—SO
to high-strung automobiles.
Somebody loves us all.

Slack's Garage

CHRISTINE E. HEMP

Why he comes here
every morning like clockwork
I don't know.
All bent up—
overalls hang on him
like some old oil rag.
Waits out front to pump
in the business he used to have.
De Sotos and slick red Buicks.

Look at those rows
of jacks, winches, and chains.
Even smells old in here. Old
hoses, old gauges, old grease.

Harley Slack can't see
to write his own name, but his hands
know where every tool sits.
Look like broken sticks. Hell,
Harley forgets more
than most people know.
Taught himself. And taught me. Oh,
he'd whisper, "Roy, be tender
with that wrench—you got it so's
the torque is on the wrong side—
Easy. Easy."

Now, what's anybody going to do
with those rows of Studebaker plugs?
Those tobacco boxes
of '58 license plate stickers?
Or that repair manual
for an Edsel Deluxe? Who's going to clean
the walls of frayed dream
girl calendars? Polka dot skirts.

Sits out by the pumps
tipped on his rusted oil can all day—
too deaf to test the timing
on a truck, tapping his foot
to the thrum of a '33 De Soto in his head.

city life

S H E R Y L   L .   N E L M S

at dawn
when Mercury
still hangs
in the west
and the scattered
night clouds
are beginning to
turn pink
around the edges

and the streetlights
down across the valley
sparkle
bright
through the rising
river mist

and a row
of crows
lifts off
out of the cottonwoods
along the river
to become black
silhouettes
over the new sun

city life doesn't seem so bad

String

GARY GILDNER

The women in the Polish P.O.—their clusters
of bunched-up consonants exploding
and ricocheting off the walls like so many Chinese
firecrackers—sent me reeling in the dark
with my three mailers of books back and forth
between the two stations they commanded,
until this hard fact slowly shone through:
neither woman wanted me: my mailers
were too big for one, and for the other
I had no string around them—string
being essential, required by law, without it
everything would fall apart during the journey
and then where would I be? said the string woman,
who moved her pretty Slavic fingers with such nimble
and lacy grace to help me understand this impossible
situation, that I now felt something like the fuzzy
combustions of love burning under my scalp.
I needed to respond somehow, to show her
this time everything was different, not to fret,
that what I'd laid on her scales was tough as nails.
So getting a good grip on my biggest American-
made mailer and then dipping into the classic, slowly
uncoiling crouch that discus throwers have burst from
since the beginning, I flung the unstrung thing up, up
and away, toward the Gothic rafters of that Polish P.O.
Oh, it flew and flew and no one at that moment
could have been more possessed by his power
than I was, and when it almost reached
where no man would ever dream to touch,
I began to reflect on a law I never had much use for
—i.e., objects in motion tend to remain in motion.
I didn't believe it in my youth when all smacked
baseballs and all spun-off hubcaps soon stopped dead
in the weeds somewhere, and I didn't much trust it now
watching my discus-mailer of hardbound books, run out of
gas and glory, begin its heavy, necessary journey
down from the ceiling, toward a tiny, ancient, white-

haired grandma, who sat, composed as porcelain,
at a table, writing; surely she had come in
from the cold with only one thing in mind,
to send sweet wishes and high hopes for many
healthy tomorrows to her loved ones far away—in Puck
perhaps, or Łódź—for indeed it was Christmas week
and who among us wants to hear about misery?
I saw myself hauled off by the Milicja,
and I saw the heading: American Brains Innocent Babcia.
They'd throw the book at me, of course, I deserved it,
a hot-headed Yankee off his nut. And no nice poppy-seed
cakes, no piwo, no luscious pierogi stuffed
with cheese, meat, or creamy potatoes where I was going—
And then my mailer came down with a great whack
to the floor, landing inches from the little babcia's feet.
Slowly she raised her eyes and regarded it,
then around till she found me,
then back to her writing as if the flat brown thing
and the man gripping his hair didn't exist,
that nothing in fact had happened—or if it had,
so what, she had seen bigger noises fall from the sky.
My fires were out, cold; it was time to pick up and go.
Turning to the other two women, I saw that
they had somehow gotten together
and were blushing, blushing like impossible peaches!
And pulling dozens of loose strings out of nowhere.

Street Litter

JANE O. WAYNE

Instead of rocks
some strange river passing over this land
deposits broken glass.

A sheet of newspaper
momentarily clings to a parking meter
till a gust loosens its grip.

Dry branches groan in the wind
and a pack of boys howls
snapping twigs like fingers.

At the bus stop a girl with books
and a man whose candy wrapper flies overhead
ignore each other.

A tinseled tree rolls into the street.
Like a deaf dog, it strays
unhurried by the honking.

Spirits

*At night when the streets of your cities are silent and you
think them empty, they will throng with the returning
hosts that once filled and still love this beautiful land.*

—Chief Seattle

CHARLES HARPER WEBB

Streets are never silent here;
still they return, faint whispers
underneath the bray of horns, the runh
runh-runh of gunning cars.

Instead of manzanita leaves and dry
white yucca petals, paper cups,
torn taco wrappers, pages of the L.A.
Star and *Swinging Times* skip
and flutter as they walk in winter mist
past rusty fire escapes and dusty
floors and barred apartment doors.

Instead of deer hiding in chaparral,
whores in skirts narrow as hatbands
peer from shadows, watching for big bucks.
At Lucky's, where pimps suck down pints
of Häagen-Dazs, they crowd the aisles,
thin voices mingling with the buzz
of freezers and fluorescent lights.

They slide through alleys where pale boys
with hair in warrior crests fight
for needles to jab in their skinny arms.
They glide down Sunset, watching hustlers—
jeans tight across their wares—
lock quivering customers in sullen,
come-and-get-me stares.

                    Unharmed,
by speeding Broncos, roaring trucks,
they drift through smog, searching
for roadrunners, king snakes, possums,
live oak trees, wondering where
is the sea breeze that used to come
with morning fog?

Slipping past winos on bus benches,
a bag man mumbling "God-Jesus-damn-it,
I'm a five-star general!" they prowl
dark parking lots, chill
on the necks of furtive men
who pry cars open like clams;
they mix with shadows in strip clubs
and porno stores, oblivious to skin.

Where are the owls, they want to know—
the red-tailed hawks that soared over
their hunts, the tortoises, bobcats,
jackrabbits, skunks who gave them power,
were their kin in a boundless world
where everywhere was home.

                              Only at dawn,
when for an hour traffic ebbs, and crows
come back to crouch on street lamps,
and mockingbirds sing up the sun
just as they've done for fifty thousand
years, the hosts are soothed; and here
in Hollywood, where white men's dreams
are born, they shut their eyes
like babies calmed by mother's breast,
and settle down to rest, and sink,
like water into sand, beneath the concrete
which smothers this beautiful, lost land.

Riverside Park

HOLLY SCALERA

It was the
   kind-o-day
      where
   flowers were foolin' around
                    and the perfume
                       came
                       directly
                       from Heaven
      pure
        passion
          fruity-musky
            cloud-spinning
                dream-singing
            honeyflowers
              baby-o-baby!
sun was 2000 volts
   pinks blues greens
      turned up
         to
            exploding

It
  was
    the
      kind-o-day
        where
          folks floated
            dogs rolled crazily
              bumblebees had zing in their sting
river
  did
    a
      jazzy-dance
to the
    mating of the
      wild pigeons
        and

Old men carried flowers

The Subway

JAMES NOLAN

To be passed along underground
like something undigested
through a rat's intestine,
this is more than transportation:

these are the boxcars of obsession,
Dostoevskian, with graffiti scrawl
so dense across the train windows
you can't see out, but sit inside

staring straight ahead at
the child molester in the bowler hat,
the rapist with the crooked smile,
the mugger with his concealed blade,

whatever the obsession, you go back
to it, again and again, daylight
doing a slow dissolve as you dive in
to the hole smelling of dirty nickels.

On the surface, an old woman slides
across the frozen tundra of the square,
neon beer signs flash from corner delis,
passing life comforts, but underneath,

down here, it is running, an undertow,
a lost river of hell, trains crashing
through dream footage of chase scenes.
A trance triggered by a turnstile click

takes over, takes you over and through
Grand Central / Times Square / 49th St.:
gulping air, you exit reborn, rush on
between the faces and into the morning.

Subway

DAVID IGNATOW

I thought that if he could stoop
to pick out rubbish, each piece
placed in his bag—a tedious job
in front of crowds, all day
the trains at a steady roar,
the lighting dim, the air stagnant—
from bin to bin, searching
to the bottom for gum wrappers,
crumpled newspapers, torn sandwich
bags, cigarette stubs, particles
clinging to his fingers. All this
without a word, bending
at the foot of a steel pillar,
it was not too much for me
to be witness.

Shopping Bag Lady

JAMES NOLAN

Half-crocked, Christmas Eve,
I offer a swig of brandy
from my own brown paper sack
to a mumbling bundle of rags
who is furiously rearranging
the contents of her shopping bag
on Fifth Avenue.

"Lady, whatever it is
you're talking about,
we love you."

She accepts with the smile,
though toothless, mustachioed,
of a prom queen asked to dance.
Out of her World War II baby carriage
come two Styrofoam cups,
wiped clean with a babushka.
"Let's sit over here," she nudges,

lugging two bulging plastic garbage bags
right up against the plate-glass window
of a glossy uptown restaurant.
The couple on the other side
of the glass from us
are having, say, the stuffed flounder
and probably talking about the symphony.

Our heads level with their bread basket,
we are going on about pipe cleaners,
mayonnaise jars, tricycle wheels

and the trash on the Lower East Side.
We are wondering about the furrier
who tossed out these scraps
of mange, which we are arranging

on our laps into a sable cape.
In front the crowds whoosh by
on their way to the next place,
and behind, the silverware clinks,
but I sit here toasting the night
with the owner, and sole proprietor,
of New York City.

In the Neo-natal Intensive Care Unit

BROOKE HORVATH

We are the children here, hesitant
to speak or touch, afraid of reprimand.
The nurses, doctors are adult; they tell us
to wash our hands, to be careful; they
say that everything will be all right;
they remind us when it's time for bed, where
dreams fill with monitors that stop alarmed,
intravenous tubing, and disembodied cries like clues
dropping amid the tears and gauze
through which your eyes, Susan, stare
blindly, your dry mouth working soundlessly.

Susan, if I could, I would hurt instead
with a clean, hard, physical pain, would take
this needle into my larger, drying vein
and have my stomach aspirated, which finds,
like yours, nothing but itself to work upon.
I would breathe through your congested lungs,
escaping this nauseous sickness of heart
that draws me back to stroke your red and jaundiced head
so new it shows the shape of birth, the stain
and strain of passage, to lift and hold your tiny hand
that does not feel or know me, though you hold
my life unstably as your own, as I would
hold yours, though tightly, tightly,
though not so tight you'd bruise or break.

Rome Street: #1 of Still Lives in Detroit

JIM DANIELS

Chalk runs like mascara
over the pitted cement
fades in the rain:
Cindee is a Hore.
Who is a whore tonight?
This cement gives back nothing.
Scars on her knees as she reads it.

Mitch Ryder screams from a car radio
a razor cutting through
the night's wet skin.
A kid slumps against the door
smoke rising out the window.
He spits into the rain.

Across the street a car rusts.
On blocks. For years.

Spruce Street, Berkeley

NAOMI SHIHAB NYE

If a street is named for a tree,
it is right that flowers
bloom purple and feel like cats,
that people are leaves drifting
downhill in morning fog.

Everyone came outside to see
the moon setting like a perfect
orange mouth tipped up to heaven.

Now the cars sleep against curbs.
If I write a letter,
how will I make it long enough?

There is a place to stand
where you can see so many lights
you forget you are one of them.

Street

para Ernesto Trejo

GARY SOTO

What I want to remember is a street,
A wide street,

And that it is cold:
A small fire in the gutter, cats running
From under a truck, their tails up
Like antennas. A short woman
With a short cane, tapping
Her way
Past the tracks.
                    Farther away,
An abandoned hotel
Whose plumbing is the sound
Of ocean. In one room,
A jacket forever without a shadow
And cold as the darkness it lies in.

Above, an angle of birds
Going south. Above the birds,
Clouds with their palms open and moving
Toward the Sierras.

Dusk: the first headlights come on,
And a Filipino stands
Under a neon, turning a coin
In his pocket.

Montauk and the World Revealed Through the Magic of New Orleans

HOWARD LEVY

in the afternoon, a jazz band
of thunderheads rolled in
playing "When the Saints
Go Marching In"
so the ocean knew it was a funeral
and commenced to lament and dance
and fan itself in the hot day
the gulls, too, set to dancing,
that quirky quick step
they are famous for
(and always do for the tourists)
and then the beach grass, never footloose,
began to clap out the rhythm
and shout
O this is some world,
hot city, hot blooming

Forecast: New Orleans

KATHERINE SONIAT

Set your speed slow as the weather
in this city that holds its streets up
above sheets and curtains of rain each year;

a setting where wrought-iron balconies
double as umbrellas for walkways,
and levees have settled for a comfortable

irony, beginning at six feet below sea level.
Mornings thicken with 100% rainy jasmine
loaded onto the sunshine. Roasted coffee,

molasses and beer quilt the shrill lunch-hour
warehouse whistle. By evening, the breeze
washes in from the invariable south—

an air at home with foghorns and riverboat
moans, the southerlies blowing in to ripple
a lake where schools of mullet summer,

drowsily nosing the surface like snakes
skimming the back bayous. On the North Shore,
turpentine groves bake in the four o'clock

shade, while in midtown perches one more
attempt at the aboveground: those honeycombed
stacks of graves, always called the *ovens*.

Bus Station: 2 A.M.

DAVID ALLAN EVANS

knuckling the hissing
strange light from her eyes
an old lady leans on
the bus driver's routine
hand, stepping hard down
into Hagerstown, Maryland
where her suitcase is
taken by a middle-aged man
who says *how are you*
almost touching her

he turns around
to lead her away
while she is nodding
and their faces reveal
mother and son

then they walk by me
and beyond
the suitcase drifting in
the gap between them

Bus Stop

DONALD JUSTICE

Lights are burning
In quiet rooms
Where lives go on
Resembling ours.

The quiet lives
That follow us—
These lives we lead
But do not own—

Stand in the rain
So quietly
When we are gone,
So quietly . . .

And the last bus
Comes letting dark
Umbrellas out:
Black flowers, black flowers.

And lives go on.
And lives go on
Like sudden lights
At street corners

Or like the lights
In quiet rooms
Left on for hours,
Burning, burning.

The Anne Frank House: Amsterdam

JOAN LABOMBARD

Wasn't that you in the Flower Market
holding the fresh-cut blooms,
dahlias, yellow chrysanthemums
like suns that would never fade?
Were you the one who hovered
by the fruit stalls
and the trays of slithery eels
in Albert Cuypstraat market,
your arms thin in the raveled sweater?
I think I passed you on Mozes en Aåronstraat
teaching yourself the faces, the faces
to the first generation.
Anne, each day, strangers file
soberly through your room.
Your schoolgirl pictures are still there
pasted to the raw wall—
the postcard of Venice, Norma Shearer.
The window you dared not peer from
looks out on a yard overgrown
with leggy geraniums.
Guinea hens scratch in the dirt.
When I came from your house my eyes blurred,
and I swear I saw you framed
in the sunset's red apocalypse,
the sun roaring down behind you
and the sky in flames,
through which you walked, most womanly,
into the pages of your testament
and did not burn.

From Poland

EDWARD FIELD

"After soulless Germany," my sister writes,
"to be in an absolutely soulful land . . .
the zloty not buying much
even if there were anything to buy . . .
the bureaucracy frightening, but everyone used to it,
patiently standing on line . . .
sweet and helpful and unspoiled." Reading that,
I think I could live there on bread and potatoes.

Ma said that from Lamaz, her village,
Warsaw was a two-day trip by horse and wagon.
My sister writes that now "it's an hour by superhighway . . .

"Some old houses are still there . . .
a countrywoman came out of one,
her daughter in the background wearing
torn leggings and a quilted vest. We just stood
staring at each other, me in western clothes,
my passport full of border stamps. . . . Inside,
just a little room with a porcelain stove in the corner
and a bunk on each wall . . . onion skins
on the floor of boards and dirt—
cozy enough to move into at once."

Ma always said her brother, Jake, the favorite,
got to sleep on top of the stove.
She slept in the rafters with the chickens
and the barrel of herring and sack of groats to last the winter.
They called her little pig, she was so fat,
too slow for blackberrying when her sister went at dawn—
Esther yelled at her for trying to follow . . .
Esther, the smart one, who learned to read and write
and kept in touch with their father in America.
He was a tinsmith and when he worked on the church roof
drank with the priest. But then, he was half-goy,
the child of his mother's love affair with the landowner—
Ma told it proudly, the old scandal, but lowered her voice
to explain why she herself was always taken for Christian.

Grandma was from prosperous Jews with a farm
who never approved of the big, fair-haired tinsmith
so they eloped to poor, little Lamaz
where people lined up to read the only newspaper.

"I kept my father's photograph until we got to America,"
Ma said, "and I was happy to see him at the dock,
but when I picked up a pretty candy box in the gutter
in wonder at such a treasure being thrown away,
he smacked me across the face and called me dumbbell. . . .
That night I tore his picture up.
I was only happy in Lamaz. Did I ever tell you,"
she tells me again, "how the milk turned sour in the pail
and we drank it that way?
There were no demands on me there," she says,
an old woman in Florida now, her children grown and gone.
"I didn't have to do anything. I could sit
eating my bowl of kasha all day long."

My sister writes: "We asked the oldest people in town
about the Jews. . . . None left, they told me, vaguely,
the Nazi time was the end of them, and showed me
where the Jewish cemetery had been,
a grassy area with trees, fenced in."

Troopship for France, War II

GEORGE BOGIN

I paint you this:
black blue for the sea at night,
black for the hurrying ship,
red for the end
of the olive drab dreamers
over the white wake.

The Capitol: Spring, 1968

JOAN LABOMBARD

So much marble and grass.
Here squirrels drink from the public water fountains.
One wishes to be impressed, and is.
The fathers carved in stone,
Each in his chaste temple,
Watch us with reflective eyes, but practice silence.
Jefferson's figure seems to brood
On the Potomac's haze
From the distance of a Socrates,
And Lincoln stares
Down the blind vista of the years
Neither blaming nor praising us.
Meanwhile the birds
Sip from the fountains meant for men.
Across the bridge at Arlington
The delicate cherry blooms
Gentle a landscape of the dead:
Two nuns in the old habits
Kneel at their prayers and tears
By the grave of the youngest President.
We have nothing for this moment
But an unaccustomed quiet.
So much marble, and grass.
So many black men keeping the walkways swept
In the city of their discontent,
And everywhere the tulips blaze!
So much marble, and grass.
So many brimming fountains bled to slake
The tiny thirst of birds—
So many graves.

This Is a Safe House

*for Anna Calero de Lopez * Nicaragua Libre 1987*

MARTIN STEINGESSER

she wants you to know,
                    even back when the *Guardia*
shot people on the streets,
bloodying all Masaya, the streets
held in the red eye
                    of the sniper's scope.
Step through her door
and let hands open,
                    the body breathe,
let the heart's muscle
                    unknot.

She wants you to know, at Anna's
you eat the cool, green light of the cucumber,
then lie down, drawing around you
violet shadows
                    the color of dark beets,
you curl into sleep, filling space like air,
moving without weight,
                    gathering losses,
old wounds huffing through blood
like blind, tunneling animals . . .

In the morning, you blink
at how sunlight
                    surrounds each leaf,
at the ways voices travel like light—
                    and Anna,
herself a new morning
                    in clean cottons,
handmaid of the earth's cup,
                    this river
of black beans, eggs, fried banana, coffee,
this Anna laughs,
                    showing one gold tooth.

Here
for Judy

DAVID JAUSS

This place is the absence
of all other places. So what
if the breeze that has been everywhere today
runs its fingers through my hair?
Let the poplars flash scatter fire
silver in the sun, the birds stitch
the blue sky with their music.
I don't care. It's appalling
how much isn't here. No jack pines, for instance,
nor honeysuckle, coral, bitterweed
or gorse. No mountains, creek beds,
warning paths. No mandolins,
love seats, daguerreotypes, train whistles,
hood ornaments, cuff links, candles. No rain,
no palominos, no . . . Oh, I could go on
but it would only make the absence larger.
If I named everything that isn't here,
beginning and ending with you,
this place would be so empty
it would be nowhere.

North Country

ROO BORSON

Hot air warbles from the chimney.
For a moment on a snowy roof
frail sunlight lands,
then lifts back into outer space.
Snow nestles in the joints of trees
like the slimness of a woman.
Look out the window.
The snow is cluttered with berries
the color of lips.

The eye that is always out searching:
what a terrible loss of an eye.
You, though, the back of your mind
is all of North Ontario,
those miles of open starlight.
I know that mind now.
Farmhouses buoyed up
in snow flat as a playing card.
A moonlit highway, molten solder.
And all the young girls, the whiteness
building up in their bodices.

Telephone poles drag their long crosses over the ice.
The horizon: peach smoke.
The tall barb of a church spire.
I walk along, following the fences,
old growth poking up through the snow.
I think of you
who left, taking all this.
Later,
much later,
night. Moon
caught on the dark wire.

Lesson in Survival

GRACE BAUER

What I'd come from was a landscape
tamed by what I knew: the familiar
barn that marked the point
where town ended and the fields began,
laid out in measured acres
of alfalfa, wheat and corn,
the bend where the railroad tracks
veered east toward the Lehigh.

Later I found my way through
cities where neon signs
and arrows marked my going.
Every street had a name
on a map I could memorize.
But in this unsettled vista
of lodgepole and sage,
there's no telling.

I go on, not knowing if I've gone
by a rock face I think I recognize,
follow elk trails that switch back
for miles into themselves.
And the mountains do not care
if I am moved by fear or awestruck
by their beauty.

My only shelter is the silence
inside I hold to, shivering
beneath the gold glint of stars.
And though the stars are unmoved
I know they'll point my way home
if I remember how to read their light.

The Place

PAUL ZIMMER

Once in your life you pass
Through a place so pure
It becomes tainted even
By your regard, a space
Of trees and air where
Dusk comes as perfect ripeness.
Here the only sounds are
Sighs of rain and snow,
Small rustlings of plants
As they unwrap in twilight.
This is where you will go
At last when coldness comes.
It is something you realize
When you first see it,
But instantly forget.
At the end of your life
You remember and dwell in
Its faultless light forever.

Home for the Holidays

BILL BROWN

Those strong young men of my childhood,
square chinned, hair trimmed above the ear,
laughed as they tossed my sister and me high
in the air. We would climb them like trees
holding on to pockets, elbows, shoulders,
and feel the healthy muscles forced
into a strained gentleness by children
who abused their patient strength.
On summer days at Reelfoot Lake
they stood waist deep, we sat
on their shoulders, splashing,
waging war into the new afternoons
and at night while I pretended to sleep,
my heroes stood on porch steps
and bragged about buckets of bluegill, bass
that broke 20 pound test, and swamp cats
that screamed like wanton women.
Half-awake, I'd hear whispers drifting
through the window screen about fast girls
from Memphis and Amy Lewis, her strut,
and all her yellow hair.

Today, I joined a family New Year's gathering
and found receding hair, paunches rolling over belts,
shoulders changed from square to round, muscles
molding away from bone like soft clay.
Hunkered around a TV football game,
they greeted me seated and turned their attention
when a referee called back a play.

And for the sake of memory,
I dreamed them standing beside a lake boat,
gutting a bucket of fish, drinking whiskey
in case of snakebite. Suddenly they pointed
at a line of honkers flying north
to that mysterious wilderness
they vowed they'd die in.

The Spare Room

VERN RUTSALA

You lie awake. The attic
begins its nightly act.
Moths stir, going through
old pockets; rafters strain
still thinking themselves
the fine bones in wings,
the shingles feathers.

It is taking you to sleep,
to the place of old pictures
and clothes you have
outgrown. In the dark
the clock face shines.
You angle backward into
time. This is the room

of childhood where your
sleeping body counted bruises
all night long as warm
shadows moved above you,
comfort in their hands,
and walked into the premises
of your dreams. They are gone now.

The only place you meet them
is in your sleep. You know
there has been some mistake;
they are out there still, beyond
the edges of your sleep, tiptoeing,
holding the night together until
morning comes. And then it comes.

Visitations

KAY MURPHY

I could have sworn I lived alone.
Now I'm sitting in my mother's kitchen
in the chair next to the door where I always sat
next to my mother who sat where she could get up.

And my father will be home soon, drunk again; it seems
he never stopped drinking, even when it was too late.

> This must be wrong.
> I don't live here anymore.

No, sure enough, my dead cocker spaniel is barking
at the taxi driver who is helping my father up the walk.
My mother is drying her hands in order to pay the driver.
I am clearing the table, preparing a place for the past.

> I am doing this to myself.
> I live here and I live alone.

Driving Back

LEONA GOM

Static on the radio
scribbles out the urban symphony.
My fingers remember
the local frequencies,
country-and-western fills up
the car like a new passenger.
It is a longer drive each time,
the landscape of this place
slowly sticking to the windows,
the rearview mirror.

    I come as always
    with half-empty suitcase,
    still looking for something
    to pack back to the city,
    never want to take it all
    and be finished

But the land forgets us easily.
My family only borrowed everything here,
the earth pulls it all back
into itself.
Fifty years are just words
we took with us when we left.
We carved our name
into a tree trunk by the house,
into one tombstone,
but nothing that will not grow over,
nothing that the land
did not expect.

    I fill my suitcase.
    stones, roots, a white scroll
    of birch

The Ride Home

JUDITH HEMSCHEMEYER

Maybe the ride home will never end.
The old Chevy purrs
and Daddy, quiet as usual,
just drives, not starting anything

and the tip of Mother's cigarette,
tiny Vesuvius, glows in the dark.

She smokes carefully because
the baby's sleeping in her lap and because
it might ignite the puffy gray fur collar
of the coat she bought when she was single
and had money of her own.

It smells like some animal when it gets wet
and from the backseat where I huddle,
the only pup awake,
it stands out against onrushing headlights
like a wolf's ruff in the moon.

Home

JONATHAN HOLDEN

A choking warmth comes piling
through rolled-down windows
as slowly you drive east
through an ancient
and dilapidated sunlight
on the last leg
of Seventeenth and past
the corner Mobil where you're greeted
by the brave little Elm St.
traffic light. It's been
here all along, on duty
the weeks you've been away,
has gone preciously nowhere
for the summer. You continue
past the bleached limestone
that is Field School, familiar
as your furniture, and turn
left on Grandview, down
this brief, dead-ended tunnel
and recognize your house,
waiting like an abandoned stage set.
The porch is peeling. Later
you'll open every window wide.
The night's incessant gossip
will crowd in through the screens—
locusts, cat fights, voices
of all your old relations
staked out as far as you can hear
in their predictable positions,
meaning that you're back
in the middle of nowhere,
and everything in this toy
and humid world is famous, even you
are famous to yourself.

The House

DAVID HUDDLE

White clapboard of course, but it's of the stained wood
of the stairwell I think first, light slanting
down from the high window at the turn, dust
motes floating for the nap-bound boy standing
with his foot stopped on the first step. He must,
he knows, pass up through shadow to his bed,
but now he's still as light itself. Mother,
he knows you grew up here, too, and Mother,
what's stalled him out here, banister-handed
and knee-bent, is that sight that came to him
from watching that shaft of the afternoon sun
from the high window at the turn. The dim
shape in front of him is a small girl: one
day you stopped here, this way. He's astounded.

End of the Line

JOHN TAYLOR

This is the end of the line.
You get out, trying to read the name
Of the station under the one light,
But it is another alphabet
Than the one you learned by heart,
And the wind out of all those miles
Of darkness behind the station
Is another wind. Still, the stars are the same,
And you turn up your collar, settle your pack,
And start. The agent stares inside his window;
You wave, shout a word in his language
As you cross the platform and step out
Into the surf-sound of grass
And start walking. The Dipper's clouded,
But there's Cassiopeia, so you know
Which way to go, and you feel like walking
After so long on the train. There's moonlight
Enough, there's the grass rising and falling,
And when you get tired, there's your bag,
And when you wake up, there's the map.
End of the line? There's only one end
Of the line: keep moving till then.

Acknowledgments

Permission to reprint poems is gratefully acknowledged to the following:

Ahsahta Press, for "Peabody #7 Strip Mine" by David Baker from *Laws of the Land*, copyright © 1981 by Ahsahta Press. Also appeared in the *Portland Review*.

Jack Anderson, for "blues on the ranch" from *Field Trips on the Rapid Transit* by Jack Anderson (Hanging Loose Press, 1990), copyright © 1990 by Jack Anderson.

Arte Publico Press, for "Going North" by Luis Omar Salinas from *The Sadness of Days: Selected and New Poems* (Arte Publico Press, University of Houston, 1987). Reprinted by permission of the publisher.

Appalachian Consortium Press, for "Turn Your Radio On" by Jim Wayne Miller from *The Mountains Have Come Closer*, copyright © 1980, 1991 by Appalachian Consortium Press.

The Ashland Poetry Press, for "A Grammar of the Sea" from *Practicing Our Sighs: The Collected Poetry of Richard Laurence Snyder* by Richard Snyder (1989). Also appeared in *The Laurel Review*, Volume VI, Number 2, Fall 1966.

Grace Bauer, for "Dancing on the Bar at the Blue Goose Saloon" (has appeared in *Poet Lore*, Volume 83, Number 2, 1988), for "Lesson in Survival" (has appeared in the *Worcester Review*, Volume VIII, Number 2, Fall 1985), and for "The Public Library as an Erotic Oasis" (has appeared in the *Mississippi Valley Review*, Volume XII, Number 2, Spring 1983). All poems reprinted by permission of the author.

BOA Editions, Ltd., for "On the Back Porch" from *Awake* by Dorianne Laux, copyright © 1990 by Dorianne Laux. Reprinted by permission of BOA Editions, Ltd. (92 Park Avenue, Brockport, NY 14420).

Ruth Bogin, for "Home" by George Bogin (first appeared in *Ploughshares*, Volume 3, Number 2, 1976) and "Troopship for France, War II" by George Bogin (first appeared in *New Letters*, Volume 42, Number 4, 1976) from *In a Surf of Strangers* (University Presses of Florida, 1981). Reprinted by permission of the estate of George Bogin.

Roo Borson, for "North Country" by Roo Borson from *A Sad Device* (Quadrant Editions, 1981). Reprinted by permission of the author.

Curtis Brown Ltd., for "Cannon Hill" by Sandra Hochman, copyright © 1970 by Sandra Hochman, from *Earthworks* (Viking Press, 1970); and for "Mining

Alice Fulton, for "Everything to Go" from *Powers of Congress* (David R. Godine, Publisher, Inc.), copyright © 1991, 1995 by Alice Fulton. Also appeared in *Grand Street*, Autumn 1989.

Gnomon Press, for "Small Farms Disappearing in Tennessee" by Jim Wayne Miller from *Brier, His Book* (Gnomon Press, 1988). Originally appeared in *Appalachian Journal* and is also included in *Voices from the Hills* (Frederick Ungar Publishing Company, co-published with Appalachian Consortium Press, 1975).

David R. Godine, Publisher, Inc., for "Everything to Go" from *Powers of Congress* by Alice Fulton, copyright © 1991, 1995 by Alice Fulton. Also appeared in *Grand Street*, Autumn 1989.

Graywolf Press, for "Rough Country" from *The Gods of Winter* by Dana Gioia, copyright © 1991 by Dana Gioia; and for "Sunday Night in Santa Rosa" from *Daily Horoscope* by Dana Gioia, copyright © 1986 by Dana Gioia. Reprinted by permission of Graywolf Press, Saint Paul, MN.

The Greenfield Review Press, for "Passing Thru" by Geof Hewitt from *Just Worlds* (Ithaca House Books, The Greenfield Review Press, 1989).

Jim Hall, for "Something Smaller" from *False Statements* (Carnegie-Mellon University Press), copyright © 1986 by Jim Hall. Reprinted by permission of the author.

Hanging Loose Press, for "blues on the ranch" from *Field Trips on the Rapid Transit* by Jack Anderson (1990), copyright © 1990 by Jack Anderson.

Thomas Carroll Heffernan, for "Mount Mitchell in North Carolina at Dusk in October" by Thomas Heffernan from *White Trash*, edited by Nancy Stone and Robert W. Grey (New South Publishing Company, 1977), copyright © by Thomas Heffernan.

Christine E. Hemp, for "At the Blue Diner" (appeared in *Somos Summer Anthology*, 1992), "An English Garden in Autumn," and "Slack's Garage" (appeared in *The Lyndon Review*, Spring 1988).

Jonathan Holden, for "Home" and "Landscape: near Moab, Utah" from *Against Paradise* (University of Utah Press, 1990).

Brooke Horvath, for "The Closet" (first appeared in the *Missouri Review*, Issue 13.2, 1990), and "In the Neo-natal Intensive Care Unit" (appeared in the *Sycamore Review*, Issue 3.1, 1991; and in *Consolation at Ground Zero*, Eastern Washington University Press, 1995).

David Huddle, for "The House" and "The School" from *Stopping by Home* (Peregrine Smith Books, 1988).

The Hudson Review, for "Pecos Valley Poem" by Keith Wilson.

Ron Ikan, for "Zodiac."

David Jauss, for "Here" (has appeared in *Shenandoah*, Volume 39, Number 3, 1989).

Donald Justice, for "Bus Stop" from *A Donald Justice Reader* (University Press of New England, 1991).

Joan LaBombard, for "The Anne Frank House: Amsterdam" (appeared in *Yankee*, September 1988)), and for "The Capitol: Spring, 1968" (from *Chicago Tribune Magazine*, May 30, 1971). The two poems also appear in *The Counting of Grains* (San Diego Poets Press, 1990).

Dorianne Laux, for "On the Back Porch" from *Awake* (BOA Editions, Ltd., 92 Park Avenue, Brockport, NY 14420), copyright © 1990 by Dorianne Laux.

Howard Levy, for "Montauk and the World Revealed Through the Magic of New Orleans." First appeared in *American Poetry Review*, Volume II, Number I, January/February 1982.

George Ella Lyon, for "Cousin Ella Goes to Texas" (appeared in The Richard Montgomery Foundation incorporating *Mountainside* magazine, Volume 2, Number 1, 1982).

Julie Martin, for "In the Garage." First appeared in *Poetpourri*, Fall 1992.

Ruben Gerard Martinez, for "Border Café" from *Border Café* (Pudding House Publications, 1992). Also appeared in *Pudding Magazine*, Issue 19, 1991.

Gail Mazur, for "Ware's Cove" from *The Pose of Happiness* (David R. Godine, Publisher, Inc., 1986). Also appeared in *Poetry*, July 1987.

Wesley McNair, for "After the Ice" and "Where I Live" from *The Faces of Americans in 1853* (University of Missouri Press, 1983), and for "Seeing Cooch" from *The Town of No* (David R. Godine, Publisher, Inc., 1989).

Jim Wayne Miller, for "Closing the House" from *Dialogue with a Dead Man* (University of Georgia Press, 1974; Green River Press, 1978), copyright © by Jim Wayne Miller, and for "Hard" (appeared in *The Iron Mountain Review*, Volume IV, Number 2, Spring 1988).

Sheryl L. Nelms, for "city life" from *Strawberries & Rhubarb* (Peak Output Press, 1990), has also appeared in *Iowa Woman*, 1980, *Horizons*, 1981, *A Galaxy of Verse*, 1982, and *... having writ ...*, 1985; and for "on the north porch" (has appeared in *Rebirth of Artemis*, 1983).

New Rivers Press, for "In South Dakota There Is a Word" by Sheryl Noethe from *The Descent of Heaven over the Lake* (1984).

Naomi Shihab Nye, for "Going for Peaches, Fredericksburg, Texas," and "Spruce Street, Berkeley" from *Yellow Glove* (Far Corner Books, 1986).

Passages North, for "Home for the Holidays" by Bill Brown.

David Ray, for "End of the Line" by John Taylor from *From A to Z* (Ohio University Press, 1981). Also appeared in *New Letters* magazine.

Paul Ruffin, for "Devil's Finger Island."

Vern Rutsala, for "The Spare Room" by Vern Rutsala from *Selected Poems* (Story Line Press, 1991).

Holly Scalera, for "Riverside Park."

Peggy Shumaker, for "Lil Abner's" from *Esperanza's Hair* (University of Alabama Press, 1985), copyright © by Peggy Shumaker.

Jim Simmerman, for "Child's Grave, Hale County, Alabama" from *Once Out of Nature* (Galileo Press, 1989) by Jim Simmerman, copyright © 1989 by Jim Simmerman.

R. T. Smith, for "In the Orchard" and "Kitchen Window" from *The Cardinal Heart* (Livingston University Press, 1991). Latter also appeared in *Gettysburg Review*, Volume 2, Number 1, Winter 1989.

Katherine Soniat, for "Forecast: New Orleans" (appeared in *Shenandoah: The Washington and Lee University Review*, Volume 43, Number 1, 1993).

Sono Nis Press, for "Driving Back" by Leona Gom from *The Collected Poems of Leona Gom* (Sono Nis Press, 1991).

Gary Soto, for "Street" by Gary Soto from *The Tale of Sunlight* (University of Pittsburgh Press, 1978), copyright © 1978 by Gary Soto. Reprinted by permission of the author.

Spoon River Poetry Press, for "Visitations" by Kay Murphy from *The Autopsy* (Spoon River Poetry Press, 1986).

Martin Steingesser; for "This Is a Safe House" from *Hauling Up Morning: Poetry and Images of Latin America*, Martin Steingesser, editor (War Resisters League and New Society Publishers, 1990), copyright © 1990 by Martin Steingesser. First appeared in *Witness*, Volume 1, Number 4, Winter 1987.

Story Line Press, for "Journeyman's Wages" from *Journeyman's Wages* by Clemens Starck (Story Line Press, 1995).

Thom Tammaro, for "Chicken Coop Hill," copyright © 1995 by Thom Tammaro.

Texas Tech University Press, for "The Ride Home" from *The Ride Home* by Judith Hemschemeyer (1987).

The University of Arkansas Press, for "The Caboose Factory" by Ronald Koertge, and for "Small Town at Dusk" by Jo McDougall.

The University of Georgia Press, for "Horseshoes. Marfa, Texas" from *American Light* by Michael Pettit (1984), copyright © 1984 by Michael Pettit. Reprinted by permission of the publisher.

The University of Illinois Press, for "The Place" from *The Great Bird of Love* by Paul Zimmer, copyright © 1989 by Paul Zimmer. Reprinted by permission of the author and publisher.

University of Missouri Press, for "Street Litter" from *Looking Both Ways* by Jane O. Wayne (1984), copyright © 1984 by Jane O. Wayne. Reprinted by permission of the publisher.

University of Pittsburgh Press, for "At the Office Early" by Ted Kooser from *One World at a Time*, copyright © 1985 by Ted Kooser; for "Bill Spraker's Store, or the Day Geronimo Couldn't Find the Scoop" by David Huddle from *Paper Boy*, copyright © 1979 by David Huddle; and for "In the Amish Bakery" by Ronald Wallace from *The Makings of Happiness*, copyright © 1991 by Ronald Wallace. All reprinted by permission of the publisher.

The University of Wisconsin Press, for "Rome Street: #1 of Still Lives in Detroit" from *Places/Everyone* by Jim Daniels (1985).

University Press of New England, for "Deserted Cabin" from *Winter News* by John Haines, copyright © 1982 by John Haines; for "Subway" from *New and Collected Poems, 1970–1985* by David Ignatow, copyright © 1986 by David Ignatow; for "Bare Yard" from *At the Edge of the Orchard Country* by Robert Morgan, copyright © 1987 by Robert Morgan; for "Lilies" from *Identities* by W. R. Moses, copyright © 1965 by W. R. Moses; and for "Shopping Bag Lady" and "The Subway" from *What Moves Is Not the Wind* by James Nolan, copyright © 1980 by James Nolan. All poems from Wesleyan University Press, reprinted by permission of University Press of New England.

Mark Vinz, for "Dragging Broadway." First appeared in *Sidewalks* magazine, Number 1, 1991.

Charles Harper Webb, for "Spirits" from *Gridlock: Poetry About Southern California* (Applezaba Press, 1990), and for "Sundown on Glimpse Lake."

Keith Wilson, for "Pecos Valley Poem" (appeared in *The Hudson Review*), and for "The Powerhouse" (appeared in *Kayak* magazine), copyright © by Keith Wilson, both poems by Keith Wilson and reprinted with his permission.

John Witte, for "Switchyard."

Index of Poets and Titles

DATE DUE

NO 23 '99			
10/24/00			
			Printed in USA